Let's pretend we are...
People Who Help

Karen Bryant-Mole

Heinemann
LIBRARY

Published by Heinemann Interactive Library,
an imprint of Reed Educational & Professional Publishing,
1350 East Touhy Avenue, Suite 240 West
Des Plaines, IL 60018

Produced by Times Offset (M) Sdn. Bhd.

Designed by Jean Wheeler

Commissioned photography by Zul Mukhida

02 01 00 99 98
10 9 8 7 6 5 4 3 2 1

Library of Congress Cataloging-in-Publication Data

Bryant-Mole, Karen.
   You're a community helper / Karen Bryant-Mole.
     p. cm. -- (Pretend)
   Includes biographical references and index.
   Summary: Briefly describes workers who provide services to the
community and shows children pretending to be a waiter, teacher,
police officer, fire fighter, postal worker, nurse, veterinarian,
doctor, dentist, and librarian.
   ISBN 1-57572-184-8 (lib. bdg.)
   1. Vocational guidance--Juvenile literature. 2. Social service-
-Vocational guidance--Juvenile literature. 3. Occupations--Juvenile
literature. 4. Professions--Juvenile literature. (1. Occupations.
2. Service industries workers. 3. Social service.) I. Title.
II. Series: Bryant-Mole, Karen. Pretend.
HF5381.2.B79 1997
331.7'02--dc21
                                                     97-20058
                                                       CIP
                                                        AC

Acknowledgments
The author and publishers are grateful to the following for permission to reproduce copyright photographs:
Cephas: 17 John Heinrich; Chapel Studios: 5 Zul Mukhida; Eye Ubiquitous: 11 Matthew Mckee;
Tony Stone Images: 7 Arthur Tilley, 9 Tim Brown, 13 David Paterson, 15 Kathi Lamm, 21 Mike Abrahams, 23 Jon Riley; Zefa: 19

Cover photograph Zul Mukhida

Words in bold, **like this**, are explained in the glossary on page 24.

Contents

Waiter

Edward is pretending
to be a waiter.
He is serving some
play food to his toys.

The customers in this restaurant are choosing food from the **menu**.
The waitress writes down their order on a notepad.

Teacher

Megan is pretending to teach math to her toys.
She has written some math problems on a **blackboard**.

This teacher is teaching math using
a computer program.
The children type in their answers using
a **keyboard**.

Dentist

Naheed has dressed up
as a dentist.
He is showing his little sister,
Alysha, how to brush her
teeth properly.

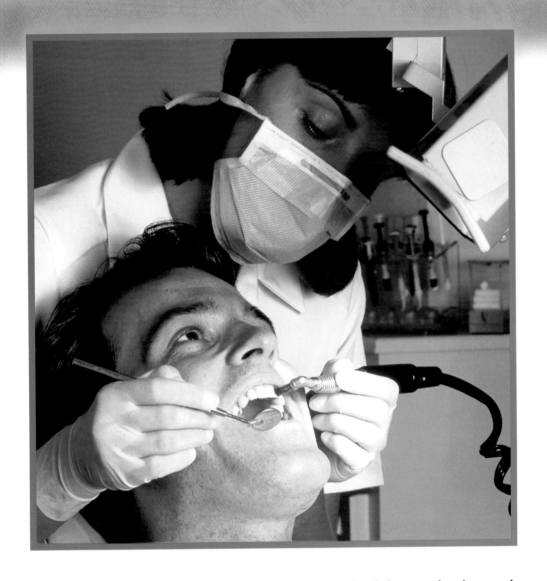

This dentist is using a special brush to clean
her patient's teeth.
She uses a tiny mirror to see behind
his teeth.

Postal Worker

William's big bag
holds lots of letters.
He is delivering
one of the letters
to his friend,
Edward.

Letters have to be sorted before
they can be delivered.
This postal worker is loading letters
onto a sorting machine.

Firefighter

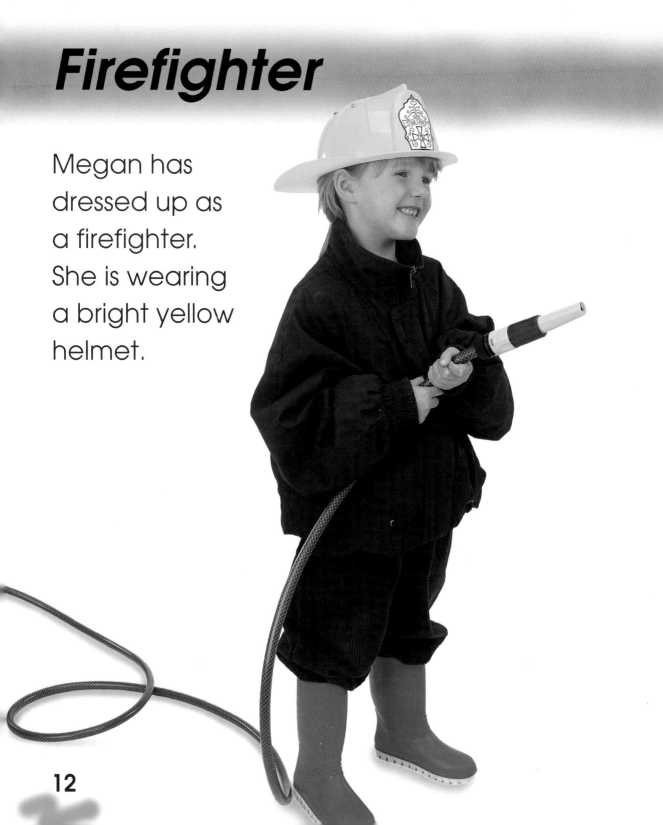

Megan has dressed up as a firefighter. She is wearing a bright yellow helmet.

Being a firefighter can be a dangerous job.
Firefighters wear helmets to protect
their heads, and special suits to protect
their bodies.

Veterinarian

Naheed is pretending to
be a veterinarian visiting
a farm.
The duck has hurt
its head.

As well as looking after farm animals,
veterinarians also look after our pets.
These girls have brought their kitten
to see the veterinarian.

Police officer

Aliyu is speaking into a **walkie-talkie**. He is pretending to talk to another police officer.

This police officer is using a special
car telephone.
Police officers need to be able
to keep in touch with one another.

Doctor

Emily is pretending that her teddy bear has a bad cough. She is using a **stethoscope** to listen to its breathing.

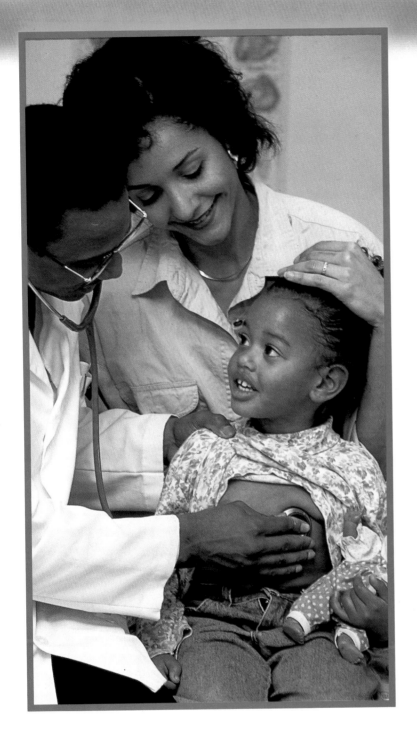

This doctor is using his stethoscope to listen to a young girl's heart.
He is making sure that the girl is healthy.

Nurse

Alysha is pretending to be a nurse in an operating room.
She is getting the patient ready for an operation.

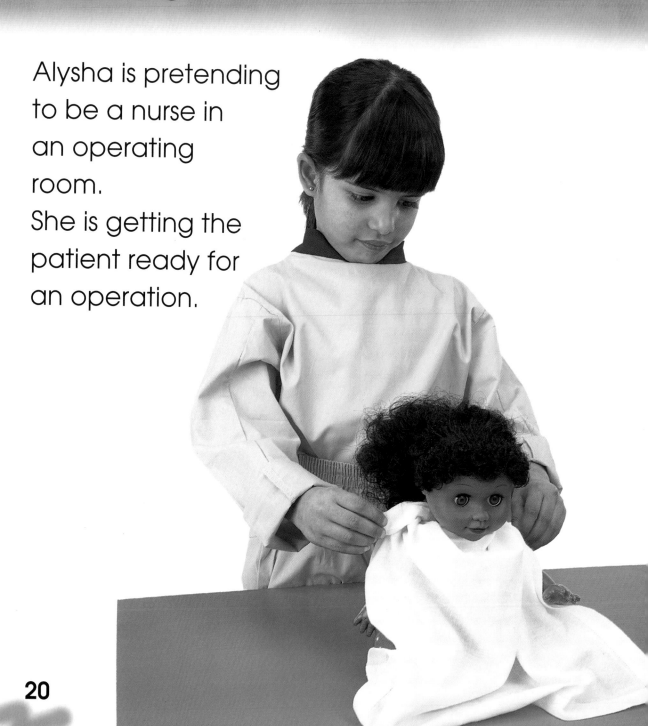

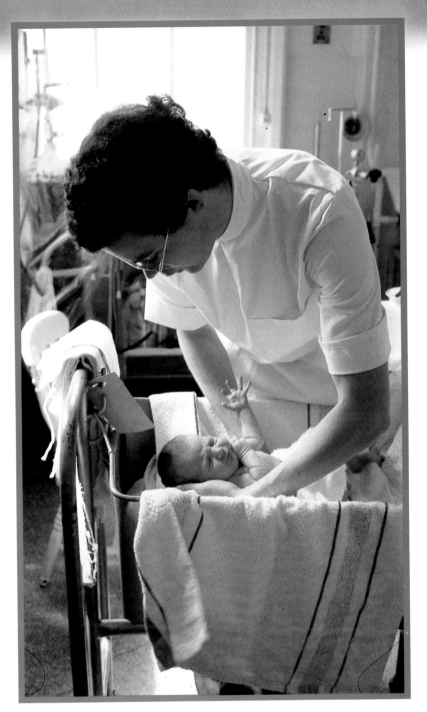

Nurses can
choose the
type of nursing
they do.
This man has
chosen to work
with newborn
babies.

Librarian

Melissa is pretending to be a librarian.
She is helping Megan find
a good book to read.

All the books in this library are listed
on computers.
The librarian can find books quickly
and easily.

Glossary

blackboard This is a board that you can write on with chalk and then erase.

keyboard This is the part of the computer you use to enter in information.

menu A list of the food that can be ordered is called a menu.

stethoscope This is an instrument used for listening to sounds inside your body.

walkie-talkie This is a type of two-way radio that people can use to talk to each other.

Index

More Books To Read

Hudson, Wade. *I'm Gonna Be*. East Orange, NJ: Just US Books, 1992.

Kundstadter, Maria. *Women Working A to Z*. Fort Atkinson, WI: Highsmith Press, 1994.

Scarry, Richard. *What Do People Do All Day?* New York: Random House, 1968.